With great fondness!

JOURNEY TO THE SUN

BRENT CUNNINGHAM

a t e l o s

35

Versions of these poems have been published in *Onedit*, *Supermachine, Aufgabe, Try,* and *Shampoo.* Thank you to the editors of those publications. Thank you as well to everyone who made suggestions or otherwise supported this work, in particular Melissa Benham, Laura Moriarty, Michael Nicoloff, Chris Vitiello, Andrew Joron, Jonathan Fernandez, Neil Alger, Shonni Enelow, Rachel Rakes, Rob Halpern, Alli Warren, Cynthia Sailers, Jasper Bernes, Anna Moschovakis, Matvei Yankelevich, David Brazil, Shanxing Wang, and Zack Tuck. Thanks especially to Lyn and Travis for agreeing to publish this strange history.

Much of Division 4, Section 8 was liberated from a soviet-era translation of the works of Vladimir Mayakovsky. Lines from Robert Burton's *The Anatomy of Melancholy* appear throughout these pages, as do lines from other sources. Occasionally I remember, as per my original plan, to indicate stolen text with italics.

 A t e l o s

A Project of Hip's Road
Editors: Lyn Hejinian & Travis Ortiz
Text Design and Typesetting: Shelby Rachleff & Travis Ortiz
Cover Design and Artwork: Brent Cunningham

JOURNEY TO THE SUN

wherein the Author recounts his travels, at the tender age of Thirteen, to the Source of All Life, accompanyied by his father's employer, Mister George Westinghouse, and not neglecting the Author's youthful opinions on the matters of Publick Education, Poetry, and Messianic Time

for the m's

Contents

"Our perversity and that of others may indefinitely postpone the settlement of opinion; it might even cause an arbitrary proposition to be universally accepted as long as the human race should last. Yet even that would not change the nature of the belief, which alone could be the result of investigation carried sufficiently far; and if, after the extinction of our race, another should arise with faculties and disposition for investigation, that true opinion must be the one which they would ultimately come to."

Charles Sanders Peirce, *How to Make Our Ideas Clear*

INVOCATION

I have reason, Love
to mention you first
not that you've always led me
in copacetic directions
no, but only that no
other power could have
made me this consistent
it's clear you make
a lot of things happen
the plants flower
& the rains rain
due to something
you put in them
science binds its galaxies
with dark matter
while I see it as affection
but really I'm no better
at saying what you are
once I thought you ideal
& endured the pains
of that poor calculation
so if I ask you now
to preserve these poems
from harm of wrong interpretation
I'm not asking for immortality
no, only a temporary ship
intact a little time

allowed at life's end
to burn to dust
you may not believe
this is me, so changed
but people do learn
supposedly even improve
yes, once I was inflamed
for these terms & figures
to outlast my private extinguishment
but human Armageddons
don't trouble me now
for my thoughts have turned
to that darker obscurity
far farther off
of our marvelous solar sun

DIVISION 1, SECTION 1

I APPEAR
to the children on the grass
my eyes dylate
& are physically scarred

& I am pointing at the Sun

falla ! falla ! I am shouting

parents & adults & children all—
citizens & friends & peoples all—

I gesture ! to the Sun !
& No-one
can say what it means

now what truly makes a Sun ?
only picturing & convening it

WRONG it is the scientific meeting
of divergent gasses
two times eleven infinity seven hundred
idiotes & artist-scholars
asleep in their dreams

ok but what did I finally SEE ?
what did I finally WITNESS ?

a thing, blurried

mark well my words; they have travelled through space

yes, all science hates Confusion
as I also hate it
but who cares, it's my living blood
besides I never planned
to be this Enemy

their needles pass through steel !
their needles strike and lodge upon every legs !
their needles strike and lodge point-first upon every arms !
one strikes my mind if gently !
4 x 4 x 4 !

   MY THOUGHT MAKES EVERY-THING
       IT MAKES
    SUNS AND
          PLANETS
     IT MAKES EARTHLY
      CURRENTS,
    SO WHY DOES IT PAIN
  TO LEAVE

cálmate, cálmate
this is not
experience

I saw, I lived, I came back

desperate to hold
my green green land
to run to its lakes
& cry at nothing

LAKES ! Not even BOILING !

DIVISION 1, SECTION 2

I ATTEST !
I AVER !

the Sun is not dangerous
for I have been on it—

& felt of its paths
& felt of its living quarters

30 billion kelvynic degrees
of Beige & White pavilions

(yes, but it is a FURNACE)

therefore I put it this way:
we can ruin EVERY-THING—
poor & rich & desperate all
replicates & starter-people
permanents & hirelings
aligned in the living laws
of the living COSMIVERSE

you can't really believe—
you can't really think—

no, a joke

STILL !
let us TRY !
let us RECKON !
& use our reason
to set & arrange
our days into tables

INQUIRISTS !
BE SERIOUS !

at five-fifths to five am
cotangent to E.'s elevation
I had my first Sustained Thought
lasting from 9:58 point 4
til 3 hours 1 minute
zero point eight point eight
ON THE NOSE

& Mr. George Westinghouse
came upstairs
to ask me what it was

& no, I didn't know what to say
for No-one had told me

trifles ! TRIFLES !
you'll KNOW when you KNOW !
you'll SPEAK when you SEE !

study the 2nd law of motion he said
& the 1st & the 3rd
reflect & convect & limit
yes it is difficult
but in 27 million degrees F
you shall understand

Every-one has their businesses
Every-one has their homes
Every-one has their driveways

yes, & every last PEDANT
will be sub-ordinate up there
& Poetry most of all

but for now there is business
& the business of business

who will witness these driveways ?
who will witness these homes ?
who will test & approve the actual products ?

since No-one will you MUST !

now one day a volcanic fireball will be born. falla ! & fires of
seasoned wood will resemble the sun. falla ! & night will be
forgotten except for book night. now while this is happening to
one side things will meanwhile be passing in shadow & thence
in darkness & thence the stars & suns will have to rely on their
immediate pictures aka the direct interpretation of pulses. now
what are they CALLED ? what are their FACULTIES ? they
aren't touchable that's for sure.

TRIVIA ! I allude to the Passing Formalities that are NUMBER !

shhh you mind
you ceaseless sound
rest you are crazy

nevertheless 4 extends from 3 !
nevertheless 5 is the shadow of 4 !
this even a fowl understands !
this even fishes understand !
horses, monkeys, & metal-men !

but you, well
you've been trained
& for what ?

TO THINK YOU KNOW !

thirteen assignable years
I checked & filled
those Measurable Things
atomic sprites & cyclotrons
illuminati & orbital colonies
rote drills of Anwar & pork bellies
encased in me your Author

& now: WORDS !

I say this is the fault of all of us
& especially those of us
who belong to a university

yes I did Every-thing—
yes to Every-one—
on time & neatly—
obedient to a burning granule—

& now it's different !
now it's proved to have differed !
complement, verb, subject !

mark well my words; they have travelled through space

my soul you are strained
you must retreat & recoup
gathering your modest hopes
for the DAYS to come
when you shall land & ahem & gesture
lawyer, speechmaker, orator

well then what WILL you say ?

that logic is nature !
that learning is unlearning !
that volition is abstraction !

you must be joking

Division 1, Section 4

thence I witnessed the pervasing of homes
& the pervasing of businesses
& the pervasing of driveways
sevens & sixes & commercial estates

how is this not PEDANTRY ?
how is this not SELF-PLEASURE ?

well it doesn't matter
I know you say what you say
from envy & a wrong perspective
& so I forgive
& am not disheartend

(besides, it's the SUN !)

then or approx. then
I looked down
& saw ALREADY in my hands
some Sixteen Favorable Lessons
in Medieval & Aquinal Commentary
perceiving their captivations
I beset upon their MISTAKES
to engineer my first equation:

4 terrestrial & 6 firmamental
2 acting & 2 controlling
7 syllogistic & 53 hermetic

& by such effort as these
there gradually materialized
a 54th thing
therein my room
floating as a SPOT

therefore I put it this way:
when all the motes have crashed
onto shores & people
millions & hundreds of times
53 or 533 or 5,333 typed pages each
(imagine the SPACES !)
thirteen years, 41 days
8 degrees & 2 churches
there will never come a WARMTH
like there is in Algebra

so, yes, now I could see
both where I was going
& what I had to do
(to the SUN !)
& No-one had ever told me

man o man
that was a Great Day

now do you SEE ?
now do you AVER ?
these are not foundations !
these are not axioms !
these are ARTISTRIES !

& there is your proof
you are scaled to Number
& a Passing Form

  ALL PERCENTS
        EXCEEDING THE HUNDREDTH
   SHALL MERGE W/O WASTE
     IN THE SOURCE
  OF LIFE
        SHIPS DESIGNED
   BY LIVING EVENTS

so, yes, clarity is a style
& so are rockets
& so is teaching dogs to beg
Some-times I wondered
what was my inner truth
but heard no answer
(DISTRESSING !)
& finished my cereal
& went to school

THIS is not a man vision
THIS is not a Blake vision
THIS is the Vehement Desire of Form

TRIVIA ! you're in a suit of clouds !

DIVISION 1, SECTION 5

ok ! then all is Hated & Hatred !
all is Envy & Envying !
yes but Some-thing must be refracted !
it must end or go SOME-WHERE !
but where ? where ?

I saw ! I averred !
it will come to an end in Poetry !

(conveniently for me)

PHYSICAL HEAT is nothing
PHYSICAL BRIGHTNESS is nothing
only APPREHENSION is Some-thing
that & the smell of astringents—

man o man !

but, yes, ok, let's say
it's all some kind of JOKE
then shouldn't my Method
be the light & airy supplicant
of a light & sparkling humor
(INQUIRISTS ! BE SERIOUS !)
each soul having & hearing
itself w/in itself
where all is heard & also counted ?

32

NO ! only the Passing Formalities
are heard & also counted !
only driveways survive & actualize !
only businesses survive & actualize !
none but science will enter the Sun !
that & the sleeping body—

well, that's Some-thing anyway

first that our minds
must abridge & sum
& in doing so CRUSH
all delicates & weirdos
up to one trillion exclusions
or, no, 40 trillion
or, no, 40 trillinium
in even the barest spot

mark well my words; they have travelled through space

BESIDES this is not a game & besides games are a kind of
number & besides number derived *per consequens* from cave-men
per consequens from monkeys *per consequens* from volcanic &
nameless algae SO THAT the mind beholding the circle would
not see its own derivation whether from gorillas, orangutans,
chimps, sakkis, gibbons, siamangs, ferals, pigeons, et al., SO
THAT cave-men could never trust Rocks to be separate, or Leafs,
or Fingers, or Feelings as the case might be, either two or three
or four as the case might be SO THAT every equation has to
be physically suffered in experience, yes, on down to today, in

the zoos and wild preserves, or Where-ever there is still sound
numerical reasoning

but for some it's just language. man o man !

DIVISION 1, SECTION 6

inquirists ! starter-people !
now we must put aside
these light & sparkling humors
& dwell instead
upon the Truth

Some-how you're solid
Some-how you progress
your mangled & harmful ideas
retract & invoke
so yes they must be STORED
yes, yes—
the human-traveller
made by its environs
BUT FOR WHAT

manageable, practical & cheap
w/in each core a Number
& propensity to damage

no! a Formality !
no! a Vehemence !
no! a Soul !

well it doesn't really matter
for this is only Poetry
while Every-where the converse persists
patient, firm & wooden

even here I plead !
even here I am being plead to !
Every-one will live on the Sun !
& sit at Solar Tables !
EVENTUALLY !

DIVISION 1, SECTION 7

having for myself
no visible torments
I reclined in a sylvan field
just to breathe & cogitate
after all that terrible yelling

now the crust of the Universe is certainly a Cosm. yes ! and
each Cosm must be followed by another. right ! and this must
continue down the line, over and over, up to the very Astrocosm.
right ! and more and more, again and again, an absurdity times,
mathematically speaking, until finally the Sleeping Body like I
said

friend, you really are in the clouds

& from my time in study
& time in libraries
I took these precious words
from the great Sun-Journeyist
Prince Freytag Von Robert-Ermine
First Soviet Rocketry Brigade—

fine !
perfect !
great !

(end quote)

4,501 bits of light
split into dew
cool in the valleys
warm on the crests
the natural instructions
of the Sun:
perfection is ALWAYS
a problem
& not just an aesthetical one

per consequens you must MOVE !
per consequens you must THINK !

besides it's your MISTAKES
that prevent & keep you
from turning to a LITERAL crust
crushed & pummeled
54 and one-half-quarter journeys hence

you know what I'm saying !
this is AMERICA !
Every-one AMERICANS !
& it's hard, hard, hard

DIVISION 1, SECTION 8

they say such-and-such planet will perish in time—
they say such-and-such star will perish in time—
how can you even KNOW ?
how can you stand there TENDING ?

therefore I put it this way:
I couldn't SEE my own errors
& so I couldn't recognize:

    1) space; or
    2) time

only houses, driveways & businesses
like I said

you think this is easy ?
this is EXCRUSIATING

so, yes, survival is hard
w/o recourse to hate & envy
I felt no light, no dawn
& crawled in a venomite doubt-cloud
sleeping approx. 3 of 9 minutes
in my sinus, arms, & blackened nails
but since I wanted it
I guess it was ok

& that's how sick I got !
I forgot lovely things
but not the unlovely
love & art were helpful, sure
& resentment also
but 3 things I kept truly alive:

    1) evidence
    2) appeals to evidence; and
    3) appeals to appeals

until Every-thing was filled
w/ warm & color'd spheres
the expressions of a root
a SUN that roars & speaks

(yes ! yes ! but not to us !)

DIVISION 1, SECTION 9

you are not the FIRST !
you are not even the TRILLIONTH !

did I want Revenge ?
did I want Fame ?
did I want Distraction ?

who knows ?
but I had IDEAS !

first of all the Fitness of Things
to be Changed

then the Moving Force
defined by its Resistance

then Cheap Sentiment
& the Crime of Religious Feeling

you think this is easy ?
this really isn't easy—

trivia ! trifles !
you KNOW because you KNOW
you're fine, perfect, great
but your THOUGHT
is yet unfree

besides, No-one can live on the Sun—
not PERMANENTLY !

DIVISION 1, SECTION 10

after that I drowsed
lost in hard-won victories
night larger & me smaller
not even twelve and a half
a glow, a path
what was important
I saw to be nothing
it could be lemonade
it could calypso
& there my mind stalled
facing attributes & types
& finally some actual
MATTER

4 + 4 + 4 !!

DIVISION 1, SECTION 11

you ask for prophecies—
I give you prophecies—

tomorrow the stars will go out
darkness will prowl the parks & atriums
with more & more statues
added to Every-place
the plazas & malls & seafloors
statues upon statues
until the Rocks themselves
run up to us like spaniels

now what will the statues be FOR ?
what will be their MODELS ?

first of all monkeys—
second of all driveways—
third of all the Little Gems Preschoolers—

COMPRESSED (i.e. formed)
by the Sign of Private Experience

so, yes, art will be important
but it will not be Every-thing
first you must put a statue Every-where
one for school
one for police

& continuously that way
until Earth becomes a statue-earth
& the Sign of Private Experience

a statue for Every-thing ?
yes for EVERY-THING !

but you can't make a statue for NUMBER !

DIVISION 1, SECTION 12

then why are the Rules the Rules ?
why are they not obliterated ?
because the Rules themselves have Rules !
subject, complement, verb !

don't they Learn ?
don't they use Discipline ?
NO, because it pains them—

so they must trap every hireling
& trap the metal-men
& women & children too
when the whole idea
was ENFRANCHISEMENTS !

I say this is the fault of all of us
& especially those of us
who belong to a university

ok ! fine !
but man o man
8 hours a night
alive & distracted
on its frozen surface
going Where-ever it went
turning Where-ever it turned
& yes all was fine

& perfect & great
though my PROBLEM
was unsolved

DIVISION 2, SECTION 1

tranquilo, tranquilo

the sky overcast
my yard & driveway beneath
set in its own infrastructure
its pilings black w/ sea-growth
& pond-scum
on the brows of frogs

over all these things
we & I would pass & travel
in our modest Eye-Balloon

pilots & gentlemen
etchers & landscapers & renderers
exactly as I'd wished it
or else fervently dreamed

my notebook !
my pens !
my charming laugh !

Division 2, Section 2

& so began my First True Report:

1 plastic magician coin-bank
1 coverlet
1 Redline bicycle
1 catalog of bras

that same morning
a ship came down
its railings going up one, two, three
& George Westinghouse
came down the ladder
w/ his pilots & etchers
smiling & waving
the other side I thought would be flat
& it turned out it was

MY THOUGHT WILL MAKE
   EVERY-THING
      MY FRIENDS & EVENINGS
    MY FAULTS & SCORES
         CHEAP, PRACTICAL
    & MANAGEABLE
  W/ OAKEN TREES
    FOR SHADE
      & GLOWY-STICKS
  FOR FOOD

single exterior golden scale value three thousand U.S. tender !
brass faucets in every bathroom value two thousand U.S. tender !
copper star emblazoned per hull value sixteen thousand U.S. tender !

the workers rowed
& the pilots rode

& violence ran
on toast & jam

Division 2, Section 3

from on that ship
we heard a sound
unshielded & hurt
& tried to refuse it, yes
but flects of sun
informed our nerves
& those in turn
our eyes

it's true you must study
it's true you must reason
coming ever nearer to THINGS
& who gets to have them
moving & burning & crying
boring & overbearing
it will never be easy
but what else were you doing

8 hours a night
dividing & symbolizing
conjugating & declining
stars & animals & literatures
famine & practice cities
& cave-men literally DEMENTED

& now look at them
out in the malls
waving their hats

then I saw !
in a crater !
my replacement !

its body was brass & copper
& hard units of rubber
a torso like a frame
glazed by the Atomic Sea
small wires, red & orange
& parts w/o decay
for all that was taken care of
quadrangals & rectangals
& brontosauri PETRIFIED

this really happened—
yes, in America—

hence the 3 classes of men
take their fix'd destinations
they are the 2 Contraries
& the Reasoning Negative

mark well my words; they have travelled through space

my legs became stone legs !
my arms became stone arms !

my arms commanded fingers !
my legs commanded feet !
& that is how !
by the Economy of Principles !

& in a way it's true
every desert must be crossed
one edge in Origin
one edge in Number
one in the Purpose to Exist

if only to see these bodies
to their deaths

DIVISION 2, SECTION 4

mark well my words; they have travelled through space

10-sub-9 A.M. over subdivided Earth
in great & colored variety
farms & cities & stringing gardens
alight ! alight !
Gold & Heat & Progress for all !

now some were brawling, some fighting, riding, running,
sollicite ambientes, callide litigantes, for toys and trifles, and such
momentary things; their towns and provinces mere factions, rich
against poor, poor against rich, nobles against artificers, they
against nobles, and so the rest

at times we gave the gift freely
others we forced

& soon Every-one had their business
& Every-one had their driveway
& Every-one had their home or model home

there seemed to be NOTHING
we could not cheer or brighten
by these acts of charity
de-christening & re-teaching
under the Sun's fruitful pulse
fixing, fixing, fixing

welcome Sixteenth Recallable Premise of Radiant Collision !
welcome Mina Rayon Duchamp Opossums Pointillist !
welcome Thistle Hypotenuse Grillers the Five Hundredth !

Double Slash Zero !
Double Slash Zero !
Double Slash Zero !

Division 2, Section 5

one thing I knew
& no one had told me
& that was that every mind
must slow & tire
Where-ever it nears its goal
it must sum & abridge
its Accomplishments
gradually tiring
gradually forgetting

trifles ! TRIVIA !
I attended your Schools !
I studied your Mathematics !
I digested your Sympathies & Treaties !
nine grades for Fate or Consciousness
25 catalogs for Frogs & Meerkats
loans upon loans upon loans

you KNOW what I'm saying—
you KNOW because you know—

but REGARDLESS these are poetries & so they have rules & so
they TRY for even faced with failure they must TRY for it recurs
their nature to TRY for in TRYING there is comfort for every
person indestructible forty zillion times up to one-million-fold
but in contrast SAYING is a poor and picayune thing Any-one
can do

& there George reached out
touching my head
in a gesture familiar & human—
he said there you may perceive
a certain thing, a disc
coursing through you
now why would that be
if you are not the true current
of the true star
gradually slowing
gradually tiring
gradually forgetting

cease you chattering mind
cease you sound
I am your chief & master

to Alpha Centauri !
to the End of Tragedy !
these were my thoughts
& I agreed with them—

a thought-tester ! an ANSWER !
hooray little child !

DIVISION 2, SECTION 6

Ocean Beach portion of Earth is a Cosm !
Newport Beach portion of Earth is a Cosm !
Every-where shells painted with their Likeness !

as I woke I ate
as I sat I studied
as I walked I thought
living in the new science
its aspects & co-aspects
wolves, bears, bobcats
grasses, rivulets, sentiments
& What-ever else
fuels the Sun

for fifty-three whole minutes
my fingers & hands ached
turning an agreeable vermilion
hidden winds blew from hidden vents
& gladness flowed in my blood

GOODBYE, GOODBYE
you deadly weights
tamarins, guenons, rhesus
uakari, colobuses, guenons
turkeys, dolphins, grit-grits
ferns, pigeons & et al.s

yes ! to be RID !
to SHED !
of ALL who have surpassed me !
in LIFE !

first: our mathematical Sun
second: that it reflects
on Earth & on the Moon
third: that 3 times its death
will occur in a Sleep of Feeling
and third (again): that such a Sleep
can possess no Core or Mote
either in science itself
or out there
in the thing's fitness
to be changed

THIS is what moves
THIS is what becomes

my Answer !
my Set of the Set of Signs !

(yes, but it only WORKS in Poetry)

DIVISION 2, SECTION 7

Some-how I believed it
anyway for long enough

INQUIRISTS ! BE SERIOUS !

your zeros are omnivorous
your ones are starving
Every-thing you FORGOT
will become your witness

for want of government, and out of indiscretion and ignorance,
they suffer themselves wholly to be led by sense, and are so far from
repressing rebellious inclinations, that they give all encouragement
unto them, leaving the reins, and using all provocations to
further them

yes ! our Rarity ! our Flaw !
our sole & one ADVANTAGE !

DIVISION 2, SECTION 8

infernal & argent airs
filtrated my cabin
but I had IDEAS
& exhaled & wrote
this my Second True Report:

that we have learned & fought
& built glass residencies
& out-smarted apes & pufferfish
comets & droughts & killer bees
& meanwhile endured the snows
of five tri-million winters
dispersed over five derivations
of pigs, sows, swine, hogs & piglets
w/ Every-thing eating & consuming the other
depleting our Innate & Sparkling Humor
without rest or pity or break

mark well my words; they have travelled through space

& every season it looked down again
while They & We lived it out
not always caring if They or We really did

shew us miracles!
shew us miracles!

I strolled its flaming surface
I turned white & even & translucent
& moreover I saw the spores of men
ascending into pods
10 thousand nine Shuttles
swept on golden winds
until only the starter-people remained

my friends—
my compatriots—
the losers & neurotics—
you Closers of Earth—

(&, really, what else are we FOR ?)

Division 2, Section 9

thence I slept & thought
travelled & syllogized & smoked
now and then a Cosm passed
then a third, then a ninth
every day a new new record

some of my thoughts were edifices
some were the vapor of lost people
trucks, computers & motels
rushing, breathing, exchanging & reasoning

but it really didn't matter
for my replacement had gone on ahead
leading her illustrious & exalted Anti-lion
her most clement lord etc. the Anti-shark
over golden driveways, homes & offices
built by licensed & esteemed workers

yes, this all happened—
it happened on the Sun—

then is the Prince of the Sun a mathematician I asked. no said
George how could you be so foolish as to think he was. oh I
did not think he was I said I only asked you if he was. well why
would you think he was not but still ask me if he was asked
George. well I said I did not think either he was or was not but
after you told me he was not I thought he was not. but if you

never thought he was and you never thought he was not said George then how did you even conceive the question. it just came into my head I replied. well he said at least you are honest.

Division 3, Section 1

a WRITER
is never an EXPERT

& so we must practice
& so we must learn

you know it will be painful
in time, in money
in mistakes & in pain
but most of all in POETRY

I was young & so I asked directly
what makes the tables
the country-sides
& the suspension bridges really

the force of forces, said George,
may be split into these respectively:
copies, beings, things & fantasies
plus movement so technically five
two being primary, three secondary
each possessed of two inclinations
the irascible and the concupiscible
which the Thomists further divide into eleven
six of the coveting & five of the invading
per consequens by association
we arrive at the One True Answer:

264 upper, 176 lower, 440 transitive

ok! then by such a law
every being is required & made to rest
two-thirds the mind receives
one-third it stages
in trains of irrational drama

now in order to wake or love
you must know Some-thing
yes, & to envy & calculate
& other things too
but I wished to love & know nothing

mark well my words; they have travelled through space

megrims
megrims
nine decillion eyes in rapid-fire

Some-thing, something

Division 3, Section 2

perched on a peak of space
the whole of the labor class
looked up at lucky me
writing these words
& cheered & schemed & hated

(yes, me more than Any-one)

but by now I had trained my young mind to its proper task
which I saw was to travel & grow educated whether or not I
was deserving & so I proposed to value the different & witness
the surface as it became depth & the depth as it became surface
during that first forming axiom four to four-and-one-half
thousand years ago & at the same time I accepted I was small
& modest & fallible & at the same time I knew my forerunners
had out-smarted raptors & apes & came to flourish in caves or
wetlands until I myself came along & began to inhabit every
tenths corner of Earth eighty thousand thirty-six thousand
fourteen thousand aeons after the travel of a frozen interstellar
bacterium & while I knew all these things I also knew they had
come from the phrasings of books & were laughable & so it kept
me in the most sparkling humor imaginable & there I remained
until I set foot in the Forty-Fifth Billionth Seven Hundred
Sixteenth Millionth Eight Hundred Seventy-Six Thousandth
Four Hundred Fifty-First Department of Formative Electrical
Education—

1st illuminated tennis courts !
Franklin Leonard Pope killed by promises !
110 DC current to 59 customers !

and there: I slept
and there: I still was

DIVISION 3, SECTION 3

you MUST encapsulate
you MUST sum
here of all places

falla ! then I will establish and demonstrate that Radiation is
INNOCENT ! & accuse it of being a PASSING FORM ! 1st
that it passes equally though Earth & through States & through
jars of honey & so also through steel lead gum or paper-treated
titanium shields in the front cone of a ship IN FACT it passes
through Every-thing with one exception and that is such
excess of steel lead and gum even scraps of paper it becomes
DISTRACTED & so allows your personal self to enter the core
& walk the surface & have profitable business activating the
over 53 thousand Westinghouse solar turbine vents with Radial
Distraction for even while you remain in comfort the heat &
light will pass you in great efficiency & BESIDES radiation
is life & BESIDES its atoms are in excess infinity millions
topping twenty topping nine or actually twenty millions millions
x-millions infinity tripled THENCE every sun is habitable with
seasonal showers of blue mineral asteroids deflected from your
soft body

yes its atoms can enter
& damage our shells
it can wreck
& murder all sorts
miners & famished & mewling poor

but they're given as well a gift
to REPRODUCE
regaining in ratio & force
if never in POWER
their anklets & eyelids gently moving
their calves & ears gently twitching

DIVISION 3, SECTION 4

No-one is bored with the trees Every-day—
nor with the rivers running from mountains—
yet they have been unvaried for ages—

BE SERIOUS ! THINK !
what is the task of children ?
what are they provided to do
that is not crying & a nuisance ?

well it must be to assemble
a mimicry of Air, Water, Cycles & Plants
& take it to Other Worlds
bringing to cold Interstellium
our love of Creeks, Apples & Stonework
& our Firm & Lawful Laws

MATHEMATICAL SUMS bore them !
SPACE TRAVEL bores them !
even GENOCIDE bores them !
& POETRY they just want to die !

fretted & agitated
they feel in their minds
like nothing ever made
this is their Rarity, their Protection & Gift
partying on chairs or on tables
Every-day, Every-week

lost, I'm lost
my left eye quivers & beads

citizens ! *estudiantes* !
there's a BURNING BALL in the sky !

DIVISION 3, SECTION 5

so, yes, time is vast
& space is vast
& by a simple leap
their conjoined is vast
while you are small & perishable

ok ! fine !

the walls now
red & soft
shields of lead & gum
even paper
bits of string & dirt
& such winds
that showered the Side-Glass
passing the speck of Mercury
Every-thing on it
moving & writhing
even Time itself

falla ! falla !
envy, hatred & genocide !
OBJECTS will help you !
BEINGS will help you !
MISSPELLINGS, FRIENDS
& plain stupid LUCK !

but only one thing
can be shared by Every-one:

TRIVIA !

DIVISION 3, SECTION 6

now there was no paper left
& anyways no surface
so I inscribed on the sides of my mind
my Third True Report:

FIRST that the sum
of 2-plus terms
shouldforth & mustforth
be dependent
& insofar as they collapse inwardly
(as they must & shall)
the outermost case
WILL NOT CHANGE

i.e. it can never be the *view*
that is wrong

the PAINT had burned away
the POLISH had burned away
& the pilots sat in circles
praying & moaning
recounting the 3 Dreams of René Descartes:

1st: Descartes is blown by evil winds to a person secure from winds.

2nd: Descartes observes a storm with the cold eyes of science.

3rd: Descartes recites the poem that begins *Quod Vitae Sectabor Iter?*

sea oats, ephemerid water
white foam & tiny redwoods
felled in primordial dusk
half-a-trillion inhabitants
built in scale to living events
silicate of magnesia, iron of lava
brother, father, sister, mother

i.e. it can never be the VIEW
that is wrong

DIVISION 3, SECTION 7

cold & air & evening
night & companions & gazelles
how far the Earth-Cosm could be
how determined in its quasi-mystery

no more can we rely
said G.W.
on the dear old human method
nothing can shield us now
but rest, diet & discipline

92 hours I hid in my quarters
re-reading the *3 musketeers*
& crying at every sound

DIVISION 3, SECTION 8

here this account must PAUSE
as it always does
on the brink of the Other World
recording for future scholars
my Ten Earliest Learnings:

7 coordinates & their expressions
two chapters on the Fertile Crescent
paragraph 1 & 2 of Sumerian animal husbandry
schemata of a Japanese radiation system
Kepler orbits & their development
inflections in latin, moscovite & slavic
works of Adolph Wolfli (critical & visual)
grammar, rhetoric, emotion, idea

Only DISCIPLINE can endure !
Only MANNER is immortal !
Diet ! Rest ! Exercise !

*I say this is the fault of all of us
& especially those of us
who belong to a university*

man o man
how we fretted
how we struggled

Some-times not even
breathing

this is not a game of shells !
falla ! the game of shells is done !
you know that you know that you KNOW !

& then: MIRACLES

the rowers
set down their rows

the pilots
set down their sticks

& NUMBER
drew us up like dew

(no ! no ! no !)

Division 3, Section 9

I'd come as far as science could take me—

the sun is a place
it really is
its core & surface
shield the Earth
it has streets & civic centers
deers & storms
& xmas trees put out to die

but some will never learn
& they must stay on Earth

taxi drivers
criminals
nightingales
poets

all the common enemies of day

Division 3, Section 10

Hear me, Predicators !
Hear me, Substances !
Your reign is Ending !

Every-thing the SUN
has done for Man
while Man has done it nothing
it brought us goats, & cattle, & horses
it lent its Anti-shark & Anti-lion
it gave the formative circle
to the airy mind
businesses & homes & driveways
& the glitteries of the seas
except for a few breakable, tameable souls, etc.
Space & Time would SHUT
so long ideas & things
& Every-one but me

seven by 15 by one third
15 by three by one
15 by one by one
15 by three and one third

I almost found a word for it
a branch of description
but fell asleep & it was gone

DIVISION 4, SECTION 1

Courage! said the flame to its night
Courage! said the night to its shield

& the little legs came down

& now I saw ! now I viewed ! & became perceptive of the facts !
that things must be as they are—that's right ! for it's certain &
sure that all things change—that's right ! for it's certain & true
that things cannot change of themselves—yes ! & every cause of
change must also be changing in itself—right !

my friend, you are wandering in the vapors

luckily George was there
& pointed into the glow
imploring my eyes to follow

& thence I walked !
by myself !
into the Fiery Locale !

I viewed my arm
in greatest lucidity
it was my own arm
but also the arm of history—

I viewed all 4 mole spots
proud of their growing fame—

my torso, hands, legs, feet & sexual organs
intact & most humbling—

every day & every minute
right up til the last
imprisoned in a shepherd's shoe
twenty-six letters
nine numerals & a zero
blue houses, blue planes
all that used to matter
petulance, rashes, lumbar—
GONE

therefore I put it this way:
I saw no gorges hallowed out
no shadows & no buildings
no people & no dawns
no globes or citrus flakes
& far off, no tents

DIVISION 4, SECTION 2

my dear Childs !
my dear Enumerators !
you have accepted & prepared !
you have assigned & studied !
at times your scores
have been graded Excellent !
but now the farce must stop
now the game of shells is done

what was it like in that forming gas ?
what became of my blood or muscles ?
what went into my travelling eyes ?

a thing, blurried

discipline, rest & exercise
that & patience
freezing, crying, burning, disorganized
fitful nights & frothing at the lips
it must & did befriend me
seven, eight, twenty, 40 hundred
no, even more

come on !
the farce will never stop !

DIVISION 4, SECTION 3

look, said George
here we are
drinking & reading & relaxing
enjoying fine cheeses
& bowls of Swedish Fish
our burns heal in a moment
& the air gives to our faces
a manner & exquisiteness
like theirs

but still I wonder
are we really happy
& not just in thought
& not just in pleasure

on Earth
they know they're unconscious
yes, they're uncritical
& such poor writers
easily flattered, etc.

but THINK—

what sort of friend puts a machine in your mind ?

DIVISION 4, SECTION 4

fine ! great ! perfect !

only 2 things
are truly motionless
they are Love & Confusion
the image of a thing
& the image of a vapor

no, that's really all

THENCE we came upon a pavilion & spread out our blankets &
began to converse according to our habit until it pleased one of
them to ask should I like to know what was our especial trouble
& I said I would & she said despite your ear-protrusions you are
deaf & I laughed & argued that her own speech was even then
resounding axiomatically in my hearing & she said yes but only
later will this reach your perceptual kernel & by then it may be
two or seven or three hundred units from now for how would you
know as long as it aligned to your other senses & George said she
has us there & she said besides what do you know even about those
standing right next to you & I saw she was angry so I asked if she
might tell us again of their wondrous system of government but
she laughed & began to recite from memory a poem about cattle

near to Mount Atlas
in Mauretania
there is a forest
that produces great number
of citrus-trees
& this is the origin
of men's obsession for tables
which women use against them
when they are accused
of extravagance

DIVISION 4, SECTION 5

not yet
are you asleep
in that mound
of sand
high upon the city

the shells
& beds of earth
waiting to cover you
are still in layers

your legs
still work
behold,
here they are

your mind
still dithers
behold,
here it is

your eyes
dylate
& your fingers
type

your hands
still perform
that clasping trick

so don't worry !
it's temporary !

DIVISION 4, SECTION 6

materialists ! starter-people !
I address you from the third largest City of the Sun
pronouncing my Fourth & Final Report
twenty-million sum thirty-seven aeons
pressed into ONE dispersal

no more calculating & happy-acting !
no more imperfect corruption of the Earth !
no more oil, coal, bananas & pharmacies !

the illuminating light will reach its object !
the illuminating dark will shadow itself !

truly there are only 2 forms
of human problems:

1: there is Some-thing left to think
2: there is nothing left to think

one hundred twenty-three million !
four hundred fifty-six thousand !
seven hundred eighty-nine !
ten hundred eleven-twelve !

all those breezes & light refreshments
all those parades & burning gases
every last descriptor
used up there for-ever

now let me show you
said George
how to touch their bodies
soft on their utters & lips
so that they perceive
our gentle message
of greetings & valediction
which in our language
runs as follows:

it's good to live in paradise
it's good to be wealthy
& spend all day in leisure
truly, I think you all should want it

DIVISION 4, SECTION 7

Every-one wishes to have
Every-one wishes to sum

but the COSMIVERSE is different
it doesn't wish to have
& it doesn't wish to sum
it wants to enter the having mind
even as it enters the summing mind

won't it make the mind berserk ?
no, it doesn't appear it will
I will enter the mind says the Cosm
but I will not make it berzerk

what about those animals you ask ?
what about the pigeons & monkeys & ferals & oar-fish ?
they too were a practice species
w/o distraction or purpose
& so became spirits or goblins
& entered the Cosm that way

i.e. as GHOSTS

DIVISION 4, SECTION 8

now my throat must dry up !
now it must stop its processes !

driveways of indestructible white asphalt !
homes of pleasing & bright interiority !
businesses of approvable plans & statements !

yes, Poetry is a luxury
& so is ratiocination
& so is ethics
& so is german engineering

on Earth you simply talk
not knowing what to say
you simply eat
not realizing what you put in your mouth
you can't sleep
for chasing of an elusive rhyme
a cigarette packet for paper
a burnt matchstick for ink

one column for children & taxes
one column for heat & transport
one column for food & repose

only an audience of workers !
only the proletarian & peasant masses !

only those building our new life !
with firmness, fire & conviction !
to spread all over the world !
should be designated the true readers !

& I should be their Poet

DIVISION 4, SECTION 9

even if Earth is a mistake
even if scale is mistakes
NUMBER is always innocent

over thirty-one minutes
& no seconds
the Sunlings taught us
their answer
but there remained this problem:
Every-thing we needed
was back there—

documents, itineraries, measurements
schedules, timings, forms, calendars
plans, statements, dockets, logics

only the said is sayable
only the learnt is learnable
learning is unlearning, etc.

Tartuffery !

I say this is the fault of all of us
& especially those of us
who belong to a university

but man o man
it still isn't done
& now what WILL you say ?

I can say I witnessed
two skies & two slender grasses

I can say the phantom
washes in a pie tin

I can say my mind was listing

DIVISION 4, SECTION 10

ALBEIT there is something we firmly believe, and this is
the history of human grammar. For early man, we imagine,
discovered himself in the midst of unfamiliar surroundings,
having risen from beasts, and growing aware for the first time
of a fretful urge more consuming than previous drives. No
doubt he felt and saw his new anxiety in relation to his own
past, which led the pure servants of position, the **prepositions**,
to call to him urgently. Forming a sound such as *of* to describe
this advance, he would have soon found practical use for similar
terms, including *in*, *near*, *after*, and *with*, until he had gradually
named the whole graph of relations he was and was in. Next
his expanding reason would have led him to notice the shifts
between relational attributes, so that **verbs** would have been
arrived upon secondly and naturally. Since primitive life is hardly
more than a compilation of such movements and positions,
command of these two parts of speech would have sufficed him
for centuries. But the ability to express only forces and relations
would have gradually shown itself a limitation, a constraint to
his finest ambitions. Ever so slightly his attention would have
separated off from actions in and of themselves, until his notice
fell upon the perceptible qualities clinging to their edges, lending
them substance and specificity. Perhaps a brilliant and solitary
individual, shrouded in history's illiteracy, first perceived some
quality to be distinct from the rest, forming in his mind and
throat the initial **modifier**. At first, he would have noticed the
shapes or general particulars of the verbs, either *slowly* for some,
square or *spherical* for others, *helpful*, *consequential*, and the like.

But later he would have brought to cognition the colors and sensations implied in such generalities, such as *yellow, gentle, warmly,* and *bright.* With this expanding world of descriptors firmly in place, everything would be readied for him to recognize the complements, that is to say the things in and around him, although this too may have required decades or centuries. Perhaps a forgotten forbearer, in a moment of pure illumination, conceived of naming his *thought* as the **noun** closest to him. This would have been followed by names for the *lines* or *outlines* that framed his field of vision, those being the portals which experience necessarily peers through. Only lastly would our subject have found his way out to the tangibles, for instance naming the *hands, water, birds,* and *trees* which he saw and experienced in his natural harmony. From that day the human lexicon would have expanded for some, while contracting for others, but whether it grew or shrunk such changes would only be in degree, not in kind. Today, we see that nouns have come to outnumber all else in the lexical array, and because of this a certain blinding has taken place, with many educated people holding that things and names are primary and essential. Yet the linguistic scientist knows better, for in truth nouns were the last entry into the life of our speech, and can be shown to be the youngest and most arbitrary of its ornaments.

DIVISION 4, SECTION 11

all that a Sun
consumes
derives
from itself

you return
you return
a hero

no nothing is
safe

not in the mind
not in the real

need
is not art

only coils
forms
& shadows

now agitated
now perverted
now incessant

besides
it only WORKS
in Poetry

& not even that
reliably

SOME FACTS ABOUT THE SUN (APPENDIX A)

for CV and AJ

The sun is bright, hot, and large.

It's so bright it blinds the Imagining Force.

It's so hot it melts the Imagining Force.

It's so large it engulfs the Imagining Force.

The sun is the main cause of shadows.

The other causes are thermal, nuclear, chemical, tidal, and starry.

A shadow has three aspects.

First there is the dark side of the blocking object.

Second there is the shaft going out from the blocking object.

Third there is the surface of the object the shaft falls upon.

Let's say that again.

First aspect: the shadowed side of the blocking object.

Second aspect: the lightless area that moves out from the blocking object.

Third aspect: the shadowed surface of the receiving object.

The sun is larger than the earth.

Therefore the second aspect of the earth's shadow narrows.

It narrows and narrows, but never disappears.

In theory it could travel into space forever.

This is because the third aspect, the receiving object, is not necessary to shadows.

Until it finds such an object, the second aspect of shadows is invisible, just as light is invisible until it finds an object.

Only an object, such as the eye, can present light or shadow to vision.

Since the second aspect is only the blockage of light, it travels at the speed of light.

It is the only thing besides light that travels at the speed of light.

Inside the narrowing shaft, the sun's heat is blocked along with its light.

In theory the middle of a shadow is colder than its edges, if not always measurably so.

Coldness is invisible before it finds its object, like light and shadow.

But coldness is also invisible after it finds its object.

Coldness is not a thing.

Coldness is a quality.

Things, we want to say, are whatever belong to the kingdom of sight.

While qualities, we say, are whatever belong to the kingdoms of other senses.

Odors and sounds, in this conception, are not things.

Breezes and fog, which are barely visible, are barely things.

The first and third aspects of a shadow are visible, so they are things.

The second aspect of a shadow, the travelling shaft, is not a thing.

It sounds strange to call light a thing, for while it exists in the kingdom of sight it also allows for the kingdom of sight.

But it must be a thing, since it can't be a quality.

The sun makes a sound.

The sound of the sun goes back down into itself.

It sounds like a bell.

No matter what it actually sounds like, it is the sound of burning.

Therefore the sun is ringing as it is also burning.

Even though we are relatively proximate to the sun, we cannot hear the sun.

This is not because we are too far, but because there is nothing between us and it.

Sound needs a thing to travel through.

It can travel through things that are barely things, such as breezes and fog.

But it cannot travel through qualities, such as coldness.

And it cannot travel through light.

If we define "things" as whatever things sound can travel through, then light cannot be a thing.

But it must be a thing, since it can't be a quality.

There is a deep problem in our idea of things and qualities.

Outer space used to be a thing, called aether.

Now outer space is not a thing, unless nothing is a thing.

But air remains a thing, even though it is invisible.

If there existed a column of air between earth and the sun, we would be able to listen to its bell-burning sound.

This column would be like a solar stethoscope.

But the sun would ignite our air-column, as well as anything else we used to hear the sun.

This may explain why the sun is surrounded by nothing.

When sound doesn't need a thing to travel through, it is actually light.

This is what radiowaves are, a type of light.

The sun produces radiowaves even when it is calm.

If our ears had been constructed to hear radiowaves we would hear the sun almost everywhere.

Radiowaves are difficult to block, but they can be blocked.

To our radiowave-ears, the blocked places would be like shadows are to us now.

They would be shadows in a world with extremely few shadows.

Maybe then we would consider silence a thing.

Maybe then we could admire its great frozen monosyllable.

finis

Atelos was founded in 1995 as a project of Hip's Road and is devoted to publishing, under the sign of poetry, writing that challenges the conventional definitions of poetry, since such definitions have tended to isolate poetry from intellectual life, arrest its development, and curtail its impact.

All the works published as part of the Atelos project are commissioned specifically for it, and each is involved in some way with crossing traditional genre boundaries, including for example, those that would separate theory from practice, poetry from prose, essay from drama, the visual image from the verbal, the literary from the non-literary, and so forth.

The Atelos project when complete will consist of 50 volumes.

The project directors and editors are Lyn Hejinian and Travis Ortiz. The director for text production and design is Travis Ortiz; the director for cover production and design is Ree Katrak / Great Bay Graphics.

Atelos (current volumes):

Distributed by:

Small Press Distribution
1341 Seventh Street
Berkeley, California
            94710-1403

Atelos
P. O. Box 5814
Berkeley, California
            94705-0814

To order from SPD call 510-524-1668 or toll-free 800-869-7553
Fax orders to: 510-524-0852
Order via e-mail: orders@spdbooks.org
Order online: www.spdbooks.org

Journey to the Sun
was printed in an edition of 750 copies
at Thomson-Shore, Inc.
Text design is by Shelby Rachleff and Travis Ortiz using
Garamond for the text and Copperplate for the titles.
Cover design and artwork is by Brent Cunningham.